W9-AZP-281

SECRET CODES

by Helen Jill Fletcher

Illustrated by Michael Cooper

an easy-read ACTIVITY book

Franklin Watts
New York/London/Toronto/Sydney
1980

Library of Congress Cataloging in Publication Data

Fletcher, Helen Jill
  Secret codes.

  (An Easy-read activity book)
  SUMMARY: Presents several easy codes with mes-
sages to decode and directions for making and writing
with invisible ink and devising one's own code.
  1. Ciphers — Juvenile literature. [1. Ciphers]
I. Cooper, Michael. II. Title.
Z103.3.F55   001.54'36   80-11407
ISBN 0-531-04146-8

R.L. 2.7 Spache Revised Formula

Text copyright © 1980 by Helen Jill Fletcher
Illustrations copyright © 1980 by Michael Cooper
All rights reserved
Printed in the United States of America
6   5   4   3

CONTENTS

WHAT IS A CODE?

A code is a way of writing a whole word as a secret word. Many codes are really **ciphers** (SY-furze). A cipher is a code in which every letter of a word is written in a secret way. The Morse code is a cipher kind of code.

Codes are used all over the world. A telegram or cable is a kind of code that is written in a short way to keep costs down. Codes are an important way of sending secrets during wartime. Brands marked on cattle and markings on planes and ships are also kinds of codes.

4

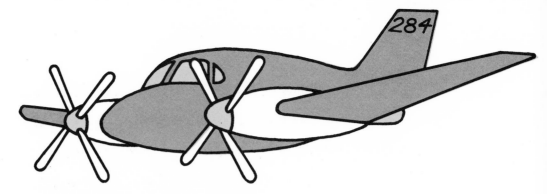

Codes usually have two parts.

The first part is for making the code. This is known as **encoding** the message. You need to know how to make your message a secret one.

The second part is called **decoding** the

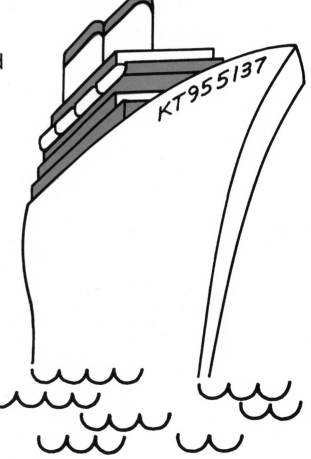

message. This will tell the person who gets the code how to read and understand the code. Then the person will know exactly what the message means.

The more you know about codes, the more fun they are. Many people like secret codes — and so will you!

Some of the easiest codes use numbers for letters. There are many different ways to make this code. Here are some samples. You can make up your own code in just a few minutes.

NUMBER CODE

Draw lines on paper or use lined paper. Print the letters of the alphabet on the paper. Then start with the number 1 and write the numbers in order below the letters.

Each letter of the alphabet will now have a
number that means the same as the letter.
Draw lines to keep the letters apart.

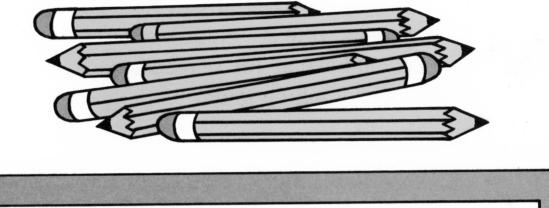

A	B	C	D	E	F	G	H	I	J	K	L	M
1	2	3	4	5	6	7	8	9	10	11	12	13

N	O	P	Q	R	S	T	U	V	W	X	Y	Z
14	15	16	17	18	19	20	21	22	23	24	25	26

Copy this message on a piece of paper and
see if you can decode it. The dashes keep the
words apart.

13 25 — 14 1 13 5 — 9 19 — 19 1 13

(The answer is on page 32.)

BACKWARD NUMBER CODE

Draw lines on paper or use lined paper. Print the letters of the alphabet on the paper as you did before. This time start with the number 26 under the letter A. Now write 25 under the letter B, and so on, until you have all the numbers under the letters. Number 1 will be under the letter Z. Draw lines to keep the letters apart.

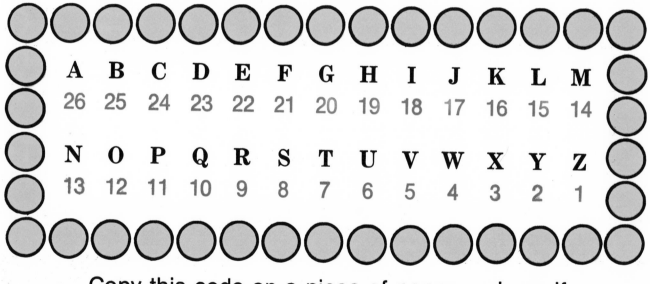

A	B	C	D	E	F	G	H	I	J	K	L	M
26	25	24	23	22	21	20	19	18	17	16	15	14

N	O	P	Q	R	S	T	U	V	W	X	Y	Z
13	12	11	10	9	8	7	6	5	4	3	2	1

Copy this code on a piece of paper and see if you can decode it:

15 22 7 8 — 11 15 26 2 — 25 26 15 15 —
26 21 7 22 9 — 8 24 19 12 12 15

(The answer is on page 32.)

SKIP NUMBER CODE

Draw lines on paper or use lined paper. Print the letters of the alphabet on the paper. Write the numbers by twos under the letters. Put the number 2 under A, the number 4 under B, and so on, until you have given all the letters a number. Draw lines to keep the letters apart.

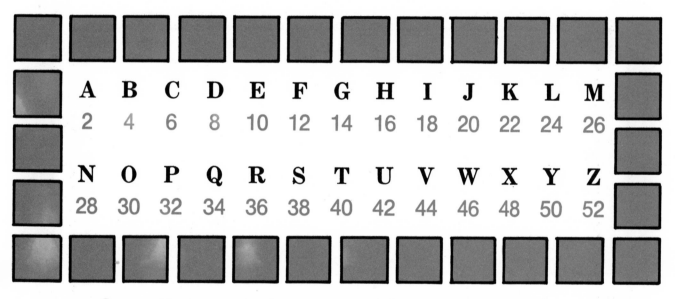

A	B	C	D	E	F	G	H	I	J	K	L	M
2	4	6	8	10	12	14	16	18	20	22	24	26

N	O	P	Q	R	S	T	U	V	W	X	Y	Z
28	30	32	34	36	38	40	42	44	46	48	50	52

Copy these numbers on a piece of paper.
Then try your skill at decoding this message:

4 18 24 24 — 18 38 — 28 18 6 10 — 4 42 40 —
20 2 6 22 — 18 38 — 28 18 6 10 36

(The answer is on page 32.)

SYMBOL CODE

This is a code that uses symbols in place of
letters or numbers. It is easy to make but hard to
decode, unless you know the symbol for each
letter. Be careful! Some of the symbols look alike,
but they are not the same.

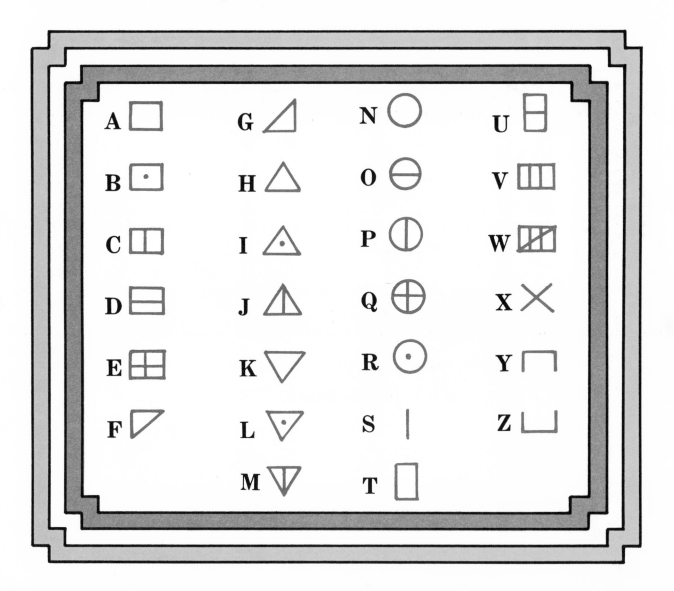

The message SEE YOU AFTER SCHOOL would
look like this in code:

⊞⊞-⊓⊖⊟-□▽⊞⊞⊙
⊔△⊖⊖▽

Now try to solve this message:

▽⊞□ー◁⊖-▽△⊔△ △○◿
□⊖⊟□⊓

(The answer is on page 32.)

Another easy code uses letters instead of
numbers. You can make up lots of secret
messages from this code and stump all your
friends!

REVERSE LETTER CODE

Draw lines on paper or use lined paper. Print the
alphabet from A to Z on the paper. Then print
the alphabet under the letters you have already
written. But this time, print the letters from Z to A.

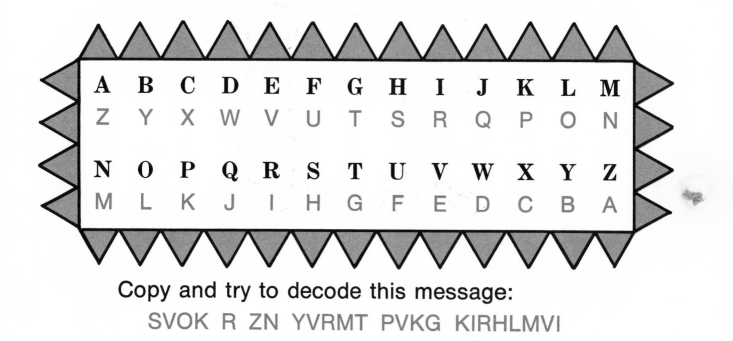

Copy and try to decode this message:

SVOK R ZN YVRMT PVKG KIRHLMVI

(The answer is on page 32.)

DOUBLE LETTER CODE

If someone sent you this code, you might be completely baffled. Look closely at the code. You will notice that the letters are written twice. One letter is above the other, and the one below is also upside down. Note that the letters touch. For example, the letter A would look like ⬦ and the letter B would look like ᗺ .

A	G	N	U
B	H	O	V
C	I	P	W
D	J	Q	X
E	K	R	Y
F	L	S	Z
	M	T	

The message I LOVE TO SOLVE CODES will look like this:

I LOVE TO SOLVE CODES

To Code:

1. Rule light pencil lines across a sheet of paper.
2. Print your message in ink on one of the lines.
3. Now turn the paper so the message is upside down.
4. Print the same message in ink, from left to right. Be sure to print the second message **above** the first message. Let the letters touch at the bottom. This will help to make the code more confusing. Your code will look like the sample.

See if you can decode this message:

YOU ARE BEING FOLLOWED

To Decode:

Cover the bottom half of the words of the code with a sheet of paper. Simple!

14

INVISIBLE INK

You cannot make yourself disappear, but you can make a message disappear if it is written in invisible ink. If the wrong people receive your message, they will think they are looking at a blank piece of paper. If they know the secret, the message will appear — almost like magic.

To Make Invisible Ink:

Milk ink. Pour some milk into a saucer.

Lemon or orange ink. Cut the fruit in half. Squeeze the juice into a saucer.

Sugar or honey ink. Put a spoonful of honey or sugar in a jar. Add a glass of water and mix together.

Onion juice ink. Peel a small onion. Grate the pulp into a bowl. Let it stand until part of the pulp turns to liquid.

To Write with Invisible Ink:

Use any kind of heavy white writing paper. Paper with lines is the best kind. As you write, the words will disappear almost instantly. So that you do not write one word over another, hold your finger at the end of the last word. This will mark your place for the next word.

Use a clean pen (not a ball-point) or any instrument with a smooth point.

To Make Invisible Ink Visible:

You will need heat to make the invisible inks appear. *Do not work with an open flame.* Use one of the following:

Electric bulb. Hold the paper near a bright electric light bulb.

Electric iron. Hold the paper near a fairly hot iron.

Pop-up toaster. Hold the paper over the open slot of a warm toaster.

THE MORSE CODE

The Morse code was invented by Samuel Morse in 1832. It is used to send messages by radio and telegraph. The code is made up of dots and dashes. These are then clicked out on a telegraph key.

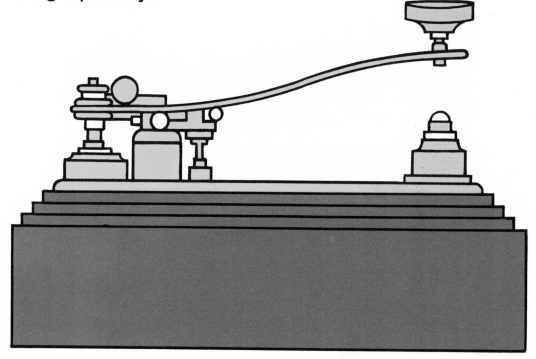

A click followed by a short space is the signal for a dot (·). A click followed by a longer space is the signal for a dash (—).

The Morse code looks like this:

A	·—	J	·———	S	···	1	·————
B	—···	K	—·—	T	—	2	··———
C	—·—·	L	·—··	U	··—	3	···——
D	—··	M	——	V	···—	4	····—
E	·	N	—·	W	·——	5	·····
F	··—·	O	———	X	—··—	6	—····
G	——·	P	·——·	Y	—·——	7	——···
H	····	Q	——·—	Z	——··	8	———··
I	··	R	·—·	?	··——··	9	————·

For zero, use the signal for the letter O.

See if you can decode this message written in Morse code. It was the first message ever sent by telegraph.

·—— ···· ·— —   ···· ·— — ····

——· ——— —··

·—— ·—· ——— ··— ——· ···· — ··—·—··

19

(The answer is on page 32.)

You can send messages that use the Morse code without clicking them out on a telegraph key. Here are some ways. Use your imagination and think of others.

With a flashlight. Make a short flicker for a dot, and a longer one for a dash.

By contact. Squeeze a person's hand, or press his or her knee. Press lightly for a dot, harder for a dash.

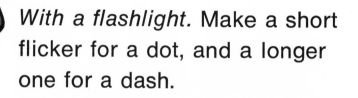

By sound. Using the words "dot" and "dash," speak the code out loud.

Now try to decode this example:

.. — .... .. —. —.—

.— ..— —.. .—. . —.——

.. ... .——. .—. . —— —.——

(The answer is on page 32.)

INDIAN PICTURE WRITING

In early American times, the Indians wrote by using pictures.

Above is a scene that shows Indian tree-writing. Each of the signs on the tree stands for a word.

In 1841 James Evans visited the Cree Indians in Canada. He learned their language and their customs. He wanted to help them. In order to teach them to read he made up a special Cree alphabet. This is what it looked like. You can use the same alphabet for your messages.

A ▽	F ∧	K ⊃	P ᔊ	U ˥	Z ᴾ	5 ˧
B △	G ⟩	L ⊂	Q ᑫ	V ⌐	1 ᓭ	6 ⟩
C ▷	H ⟨	M ᑊ	R ○	W ⌐	2 Ꮐ	7 ⟨
D ◁	I ∪	N ᒥ	S ᐟ	X ∟	3 ᓀ	8 ⟩
E ∨	J ∩	O ᒍ	T ᑊ	Y ᔦ	4 ᓂ	9 ᒡ

See if you can decode this Cree message.

ᑫᑊᒍ⊃∨ ᑊ∨▽ᒥᑫ ∧∪○∨

(The answer is on page 32.)

MAKE UP YOUR OWN CODE!

You can make up your own code using this kind of sign. All you need to do is copy the letters from A to Z and the numbers from 1 to 9. Then make up a symbol for each letter and number. This symbol will stand for the letter but will not be the same as the letter. Then you can send messages in your own code!

UP-DOWN CODE

If you were given this jumble of letters, you would surely be puzzled:

DNEOSHNSOLHPEIYURNTAEU
AGRUTIGCUDAPNFOAEOCRFL

You might think someone had pulled letters out of a bag.

But you would be wrong. This is a real message written in a real code.

The message is:

Dangerous things could happen if you are not careful

To Code:

1. Print your message on one line on a piece of

paper. Do not leave any space between the words. It will look like this:

DANGEROUSTHINGSCOULDHAPPENIFYOUARENOTCAREFUL

2. This time print the message with the first letter of the first word on one line. Then put the second letter of the first word on the line beneath it. Next to the first letter, print the third letter of the word. Beneath it, print the fourth letter. Do this with the entire message. Put one letter up, the next letter down, until the code is finished.

To Decode:

Print the letters in a line, taking one letter from the top line and the next letter from the bottom line, in order.

On a piece of paper, see if you can find out what is written here:

MEMATRHGMUDRHBIGADEILAEERTLN
ETEFETEAENETERDENWWLMKSCEPAS

(The answer is on page 32.)

TIC-TAC-TOE CODE

Tic-tac-toe is a very popular pencil-and-paper game. This code comes from the nine sections of the tic-tac-toe box. Tic-tac-toe is also called "naughts and crosses."

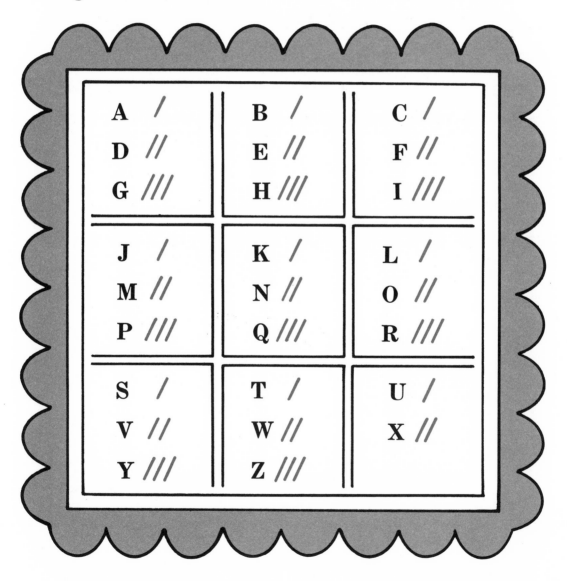

Each set of slanted lines /, //, and ///, placed in each of the nine boxes, shows which letter the slanted line stands for. For example, the letter A is ⟋⟍, the letter B is ⟍⟋, and the letter C ⟍⟋. Use dashes between words.

The message TIC-TAC-TOE AWAY WE GO would look like this in code:

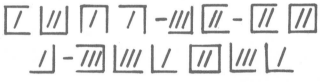

See if you can decode this message:

(The answer is on page 32.)

This code can also be used with dots replacing the slanted lines to show the letters. It is a well-known code called the Masonic cipher. During the Civil War in the United States, it was used by Northern prisoners in Confederate prisons to give messages to friends on the outside.

SQUARE BOX CODE

Draw a large square on a piece of paper with a pencil and ruler. Divide the square into 25 smaller squares. You can fit the 26 letters of the alphabet into the 25 squares by putting two letters in one of the squares. W and X would be good ones to put in one square.

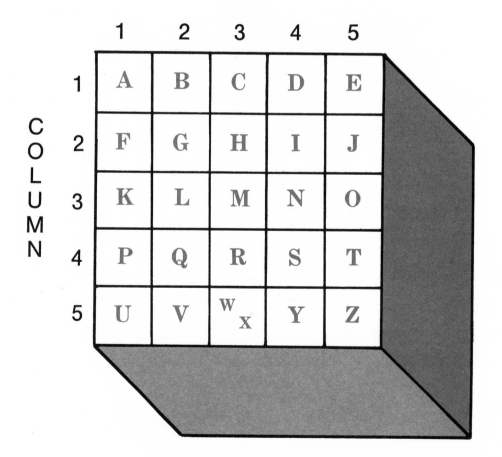

This code uses numbers in place of letters. The code for A is 11, because A is in the first (1) column and the first (1) row. The code for M would be 33, because it appears in the third (3) column and the third (3) row. Always use your column number first.

Read *across* for rows, and read *down* for columns. Put dashes between the words.

The message RUN FOR HELP would look like this:

43 51 34 — 21 35 43 — 23 15 32 41

Here is a message to copy and decode:

44 51 44 11 34 — 24 44 — 33 54 —
12 15 44 45 — 21 43 24 15 34 14

(The answer is on page 32.)

WINDOW CODE

This code is almost like playing a game. But it needs some planning. Suppose you want to share a secret with someone. You can do this by sending a message *within* a message. Take a look at Mary's note to Bill. It looks very simple.

DEAR BILL,
I WOULD LOVE TO HAVE A NEW BICYCLE
LIKE THE ONE YOU HAVE. I'D BE HAPPY
TO SPEND A LOT OF TIME TRYING TO
GET MONEY TO BUY ONE.
                    YOUR FRIEND,
                    MARY

But hidden in this harmless message is another message, a *secret* one.

So that Bill would be able to decode the message, Mary had to make a pattern, or stencil. She placed another piece of paper on top of the note and held them up to the light. With a pencil she drew outlines around just those words that make up the secret message. Then she cut them

out with her scissors to make little windows.
The pattern looked like this:

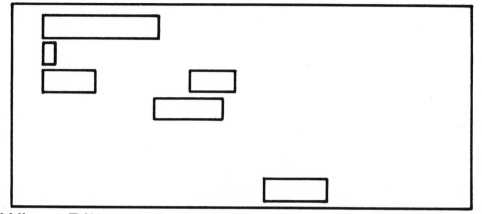

When Bill put the pattern over the note, he was able to read Mary's Valentine to him.

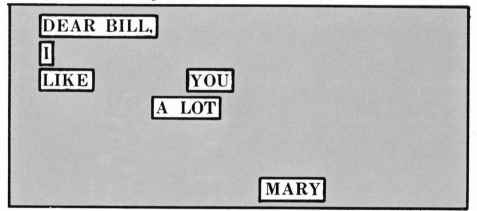

(Be sure to send the note and the pattern *separately.* If you send them together, they might fall into enemy hands!)

Keep the pattern you have and make up a new message and code to fit the pattern.

ANSWERS

page 7.   My name is Sam.

page 8.   Let's play ball after school.

page 9.   Bill is nice but Jack is nicer.

page 11.   Let's go fishing today.

page 12.   Help. I am being kept prisoner.

page 19.   What hath God wrought?

page 20.   I think Audrey is pretty.

page 22.   Smoke means fire.

page 25.   Meet me after the game under the bridge
and we will make secret plans.

page 27.   Let's go on a picnic.

page 29.   Susan is my best friend.